ARE YOU ON THE R.I.G.H.T. TRACK?

A Guide To Finding Your Path In Life

Benjamin M. Noynay

BMN Publishing

Copyright © 2025 by Benjamin M. Noynay

All rights reserved.

No portion of this book may be reproduced in any form without written permission from the publisher or author, except as permitted by U.S. copyright law.

This publication is designed to provide accurate and authoritative information in regard to the subject matter covered. It is sold with the understanding that neither the author nor the publisher is engaged in rendering legal, investment, accounting or other professional services. While the publisher and author have used their best efforts in preparing this book, they make no representations or warranties with respect to the accuracy or completeness of the contents of this book and specifically disclaim any implied warranties of merchantability or fitness for a particular purpose. No warranty may be created or extended by sales representatives or written sales materials. The advice and strategies contained herein may not be suitable for your situation. You should consult with a professional when appropriate. Neither the publisher nor the author shall be liable for any loss of profit or any other commercial damages, including but not limited to special, incidental, consequential, personal, or other damages.

Book Cover by BMN Graphics

First edition 2025

Contents

INTRODUCTION	V
1. Understanding Your Values	1
2. Identifying Your Strengths	9
3. Creating a Vision for Your Future	21
4. Setting Goals	33
5. Overcoming Obstacles	47
6. Adjusting Your Course	59
7. Embracing Change and Uncertainty	67
8. Measuring Success and Redefining Progress	73
9. Building a Support System for Your Journey	81
10. Staying Aligned with Your True Self	89
CONCLUSION	95
Final Thoughts	97
About the author	99

INTRODUCTION

Have you ever felt lost or unsure of where you're headed in life? Do you feel as though you're merely passing through life without making any significant progress towards your goals? If so, you're not alone. Many individuals grapple with navigating their path and maintaining a sense of direction. But you can take steps to find your way to a happy life.

The journey towards finding the right track in life can be a challenging and sometimes overwhelming process. Many people have trouble deciding what to do with their lives, where to go, and how to get there. They may feel stuck or unsure of how to move forward.

However, it's important to remember that finding the right track is a personal journey that requires self-reflection, self-awareness, and a willingness to take action. It's about discovering what truly matters to you, identifying your strengths and values, and aligning your goals with your vision for the future.

This book is designed to guide you through the process of finding your path and staying on track towards a fulfilling life. Each chapter will provide practical tools and exercises to help you gain clarity on your values and strengths, create a vision for your future, set achievable goals, and overcome obstacles along the way.

This book will help you find the right path and stay on it, whether you're just starting out or feeling lost. With commitment, self-reflection, and the right tools, you can discover your path and create a life that aligns with your purpose and values.

THE ACRONYM R.I.G.H.T.

The acronym **R.I.G.H.T.** stands for **R**espect, **I**ntegrity, **G**ratitude, **H**onesty, and **T**rust. These five values are essential for building strong and positive relationships with others and for creating a better world for ourselves.

1. Respect: Respect involves treating others with dignity, empathy, and understanding. It means that we value their opinions, beliefs, and experiences, even if they are different from ours. Respect is essential in promoting social justice, equality, and diversity.

2. **Integrity:** Integrity involves acting with honesty,

fairness, and accountability in our interactions with others. It means that we adhere to our moral and ethical principles and do not compromise our values for personal gain or benefit. Integrity is essential in building trust, credibility, and reputation.

3. **Gratitude:** Gratitude involves expressing appreciation, thankfulness, and kindness towards others. It means that we recognize the contributions and efforts of others and acknowledge the positive aspects of our lives. Gratitude is essential in promoting happiness, well-being, and positive emotions.

4. **Honesty:** Honesty involves being truthful, transparent, and reliable in our interactions with others. It means that we do not deceive or mislead others for personal gain or benefit. Honesty is essential in building trust, credibility, and respect.

5. **Trust:** Trust involves relying on and having confidence in others to act in a trustworthy and reliable manner. It means that we believe that others will act with integrity, honesty, and fairness in their interactions with us. Trust is essential in building positive relationships, promoting cooperation, and achieving common goals.

The acronym R.I.G.H.T. represents the five values mentioned above that are essential in promoting positive relationships in business and family environments. By practicing these values in our daily lives, we can foster and create a better world for ourselves and for the future generations.

Chapter 1

Understanding Your Values

In the journey of life, being "on the right track" isn't about following someone else's map or fulfilling societal expectations. It's about understanding your own internal compass—the values that define who you are, what matters to you, and how you want to live. Your values are the foundation for every decision you make, every goal you pursue, and every step you take. They are the bedrock of your fulfillment, guiding you even when the path ahead is unclear.

Without clarity about your values, it's easy to get swept up in the currents of life, following trends, chasing external validation, or pursuing goals that don't align with your true self. On the other hand, when you're deeply connected to your values, you can navigate challenges with confidence, find meaning in the ordinary, and experience a greater sense of purpose. This chapter focuses on identifying and embracing the core values that will guide you on your journey ahead.

1. What Are Values?

Values are the deeply held beliefs that shape your behavior, decisions, and the way you view the world. They are the principles and standards that you hold as most important in your life. Unlike goals, which are destinations or specific achievements, values are more abstract and long-lasting. They are like the roots of a tree, giving you stability and nourishment even as the seasons of life change.

For some, values might include things like honesty, loyalty, family, creativity, personal growth, or social justice. For others, values might revolve around independence, adventure, community, or spirituality. Whatever your values are, they are deeply personal and unique to you. The important thing is that they align with who you truly are and what brings you fulfillment.

Identifying your values can sometimes feel challenging, especially if you've spent much of your life adhering to external expectations or conforming to societal norms. This chapter will guide you through the process of uncovering your core values, helping you to recognize the principles that resonate most deeply with you.

2. Why Values Matter

Values hold significance as they guide you towards the life that brings you the most fulfillment and meaning. When you live in alignment with your values, you experience a sense of integrity and inner harmony. On the other hand, when your actions and choices conflict with your values, you may feel a sense of dissatisfaction, frustration, or even emptiness.

For example, if one of your core values is creativity, but you're stuck in a rigid, monotonous job that doesn't allow for creative expression, you may feel drained or disconnected from yourself. Similarly, if you value family but spend most of your time and energy focused on work at the expense of relationships, you may feel a growing sense of imbalance in your life.

Living by your values helps you make clearer decisions and move closer to the life you want. Instead of feeling conflicted or pulled in different directions, you'll have a clear sense of what matters most, making it easier to prioritize your time and energy. Knowing your values helps you say "yes" to what truly aligns with your heart and "no" to distractions or pressures that pull you away from your true path.

3. The Impact of Misaligned Values

When you live out of alignment with your values—whether consciously or unconsciously—the effects can be far-reaching. You may find yourself feeling restless, unfulfilled, or constantly striving for something that never seems to materialize. This is often because you're working toward goals that don't reflect your true self or following a path that isn't yours.

For instance, many people pursue careers or life paths that they believe will bring them success, financial security, or societal approval, only to find themselves feeling empty or disconnected from their purpose. This misalignment can lead to chronic stress, dissatisfaction, and a lack of motivation. On the surface, everything may appear to be "going well," but internally, there's a nagging sense that something is missing.

The key to real fulfillment is identifying what's missing and reconnecting with your values. When you feel unhappy or burnt out, it's time to refocus on what matters most. By bringing your life back into alignment with your values, you can regain a sense of direction and purpose.

4. Identifying Your Core Values

So, how do you begin to uncover your values? The process starts with reflection. Here are some exercises that can help you identify the core values that are most important to you:

Exercise 1: Reflect on Peak Moments

- Think back to times in your life when you felt most alive, fulfilled, or proud. These moments could be personal or professional, big or small. What was happening during these times? What values were you expressing or living out? Perhaps you were helping someone in need, creating something new, spending quality time with loved ones, or standing up for a cause you believe in. The values present in these peak moments are likely to be some of your core values.

Exercise 2: Identify What Frustrates You

- Sometimes, identifying your values is easier when you think about what frustrates or angers you. What situations or behaviors trigger strong negative emotions for you? For example, if dishonesty or injustice deeply upsets you, it could be a sign that integrity or fairness is one of your core values. Frustrations often highlight where there is a mismatch between what you value and what you're experiencing.

Exercise 3: List Your Non-Negotiables

- Another way to uncover your values is to think

about what you consider "non-negotiable" in your life. What are the principles you refuse to compromise on, no matter the situation? These are the aspects of your life that are most important to you, whether it's maintaining your freedom, practicing compassion, or prioritizing family.

Exercise 4: Consider Your Role Models
- Who are the people you admire most, and why? Often, the qualities we admire in others reflect the values we hold within ourselves. Whether it's a public figure, a mentor, or a close friend, think about the values these individuals embody and how they resonate with you.

5. Prioritizing and Defining Your Values

After completing these exercises, you might have a long list of potential values, but how do you narrow it down to the ones that matter most? It's important to prioritize your values so that you can focus on those that will have the greatest impact on your life.

Start by reviewing your list and circling the values that resonate most strongly with you. These should be the values that feel essential to your sense of fulfillment and purpose. Once you have your top values, define what each one means to you personally. For example, if "freedom" is one of your values, what does freedom look like in your life? Is it the ability to make your own decisions, the flexibility to pursue your passions, or the freedom from societal expectations?

By defining your values in a way that is personal and meaningful, you give them greater clarity and power. You'll also find it easier to recognize when you're living in alignment with them—and when you're not.

6. Living in Alignment with Your Values

Now that you've identified your core values, the next step is to begin integrating them into your daily life. This is where the real transformation happens. Start by reflecting on your current life and how well it aligns with your values. Are there areas where you feel out of alignment? What changes could you make to bring your life closer to your values?

Living in alignment with your values doesn't require drastic life changes overnight. Often, it's about making small, meaningful adjustments. For instance, if "family" is a core value, you might prioritize spending more quality time with loved ones, even if it means adjusting your work schedule or setting stronger boundaries with your time. If "creativity" is a value, you might carve out space in your day for creative pursuits, even if they don't directly contribute to your career.

As you make these adjustments, you'll notice a shift. When your actions align with your values, you'll feel more energized, focused, and fulfilled. Living according to your values will naturally guide you toward the life that's right for you over time.

Understanding your values is the foundation of being on the right track in life. These values serve as guideposts, helping you navigate decisions, set goals, and live a life that feels authentic and fulfilling. Keep your values at the forefront of your life as you progress. These values will act as your compass, guiding you on a path that is uniquely yours.

In the next chapter, we'll explore how to identify and leverage your unique strengths—another essential element of finding and staying on the right track. Together, your values and strengths will create a powerful combination that helps you live a life of purpose and meaning.

Chapter 2

Identifying Your Strengths

As we continue the journey of discovering whether you're on the right track in life, it's essential to focus on a key aspect of self-awareness: understanding your strengths.

Your strengths are the natural abilities, talents, and skills that come effortlessly to you, and when used effectively, they can propel you toward success, fulfillment, and alignment with your purpose. When you play to your strengths, you maximize your potential, achieve more with less struggle, and experience a greater sense of satisfaction in your work and personal life.

This chapter will teach you how to find your strengths, why they matter, and how to use them to stay on track. By the end of this chapter, you'll know what makes you unique and how to use it in your daily life.

1. What Are Strengths?

Strengths are the natural talents, skills, and abilities that allow you to excel in specific areas. Unlike learned skills, which you can develop over time, your strengths are often inherent qualities that feel instinctive and intuitive. They are the things you do well without even thinking about it—the activities that make you feel confident and energized.

For example, some people are naturally excellent problem-solvers, able to break down complex issues and find creative solutions quickly. Others may excel in communication, easily connecting with people and expressing ideas clearly. Still others might have a knack for leadership, organizing teams, and motivating others toward a common goal.

Strengths come in many forms, and they don't always have to fit into traditional categories like technical skills or job-related abilities. Some of the most powerful strengths are qualities like empathy, resilience, adaptability, or intuition. The key is to recognize what makes you uniquely effective in different situations.

2. The Power of Knowing Your Strengths

Understanding your strengths plays a crucial role in choosing the right path in life. When you focus on your strengths, you're more likely to experience "flow"—a state of heightened focus and immersion where you're fully engaged and at your best. During these moments, time seems to pass quickly, and the work feels rewarding rather than exhausting.

Knowing your strengths helps you make choices that let you do what you do best. Whether you're choosing a career path, selecting projects to work on, or deciding how to spend your spare time, prioritizing activities that align with your strengths increases your chances of success and fulfillment.

On the flip side, when you focus on your weaknesses—trying to improve areas that don't come naturally to you—you often end up frustrated, exhausted, and disengaged. That doesn't mean you should ignore your weaknesses entirely, but you'll achieve more by amplifying your strengths rather than spending excessive time trying to fix what isn't working.

3. The Difference Between Skills and Strengths

It's important to distinguish between strengths and learned skills. Skills are abilities that you acquire over time through practice, training, or education. For example, you might develop skills in public speaking, computer programming, or graphic design through study and effort. Skills are important, but they aren't always your natural strengths.

Your strengths, on the other hand, are the innate talents and qualities that are part of who you are. While skills can complement your strengths, your strengths are often what make you stand out in a particular area. For example, two people might both develop the skill of public speaking, but one might have a natural strength in storytelling or captivating an audience, while the other might excel in structuring logical arguments.

To truly excel, it's essential to align your learned skills with your natural strengths. When you can combine what you've learned with what you naturally do well, you create a powerful combination that sets you apart and helps you achieve more with greater ease.

4. How to Identify Your Strengths

Identifying your strengths requires a combination of self-reflection, feedback from others, and observation of your behaviors and experiences. Here are several exercises to help you uncover your unique strengths:

Exercise 1: Reflect on Past Successes

- Think back to moments in your life when you felt proud of an achievement or experienced success. What were you doing in those moments? What strengths were you using? These could be moments from your career, personal life, or even hobbies where you felt confident and capable. By analyzing these experiences, you can identify patterns that point to your strengths.

- For example, if you consistently find that you've excelled in team projects or group settings, you might have strengths in collaboration or leadership. If you've achieved success in creative endeavors, you might have strengths in innovation or problem-solving.

Exercise 2: Pay Attention to Flow States

- As mentioned earlier, a "flow state" is a mental state where you're fully absorbed in an activity, losing track of time and feeling deeply engaged. Reflect on the activities where you've experienced this sense of flow. What were you doing during these moments? These activities often reveal your strengths because they come naturally to you and bring you a sense of enjoyment.

- For example, you might experience flow when solving complex problems, organizing a project, or helping others navigate challenges. Flow states often highlight where your strengths lie because they show you the areas where you're most effective and energized.

Exercise 3: Ask for Feedback

- Sometimes it can be difficult to see our own strengths because they feel so natural to us that we assume everyone else has the same abilities. Asking for feedback from others—whether friends, family members, colleagues, or mentors—can offer helpful information about the strengths you may not have fully recognized.

- Ask those around you what they think you do particularly well, or when they've seen you at your best. Often, others can see patterns in your behavior or abilities that you might overlook. Their feedback can provide a fresh perspective on your natural talents.

Exercise 4: Take a Strengths Assessment

- If you're looking for a more structured approach to identifying your strengths, consider taking a strengths assessment. One well-known tool is the CliftonStrengths assessment (formerly known as StrengthsFinder), which helps individuals identify their top strengths in areas such as relationship-building, influencing, strategic thinking, and execution. There are many other assessments available as well, and they can provide a helpful framework for understanding your unique abilities.

- While assessments are valuable tools, it's important to keep in mind that they're only one aspect of the whole picture. Combine the results with your own reflections and feedback from others to get a comprehensive view of your strengths.

5. Leveraging Your Strengths

Once you've identified your strengths, the next step is learning how to leverage them in your daily life. Here are some strategies for using your strengths more effectively:

a. Align Your Career with Your Strengths

- One of the most impactful ways to stay on the right track is to choose a career or work environment that allows you to use your strengths regularly. If you're currently in a job that doesn't align with your strengths, it may be time to consider a career shift or, at the very least, find ways to incorporate your strengths into your current role.

- For example, if you excel at communication but find yourself in a role that requires more solitary work, seek opportunities to present ideas, collaborate with colleagues, or lead meetings. If problem-solving is your strength, volunteer for projects that involve troubleshooting complex issues or developing new strategies.

b. Focus on Strength-Based Goals

- When setting goals for yourself, focus on how you can use your strengths to achieve them. Instead of trying to improve areas where you're weak, set goals that allow you to leverage what you naturally do well. This doesn't mean you should ignore areas for improvement, but prioritize goals that align with your core abilities.

- For instance, if you're naturally good at building relationships, focus on networking, collaboration, or mentorship as part of your professional development. If you have a strength in creativity, set goals related to innovation, new projects, or creative problem-solving.

c. Build a Strengths-Based Routine

- Another way to leverage your strengths is to build them into your daily routine. Structure your day in a way that allows you to spend more time doing the activities that align with your strengths. For example, if your strength is focus, carve out uninterrupted blocks of time to work on projects that require deep concentration. If your strength is empathy, make time to connect with colleagues, friends, or clients in meaningful ways.

- By integrating your strengths into your daily life, you'll experience more fulfillment and productivity. When you align your most enjoyable tasks with your strengths, they will come more naturally to you.

d. Collaborate with Others to Complement Strengths

- No one is great at everything, and that's okay. Working with others who have complementary strengths is one of the best ways to stay on track. This lets you focus on your strengths while relying on others for your weaknesses.

- For example, if you're great at big-picture thinking but struggle with the details, collaborate with someone who excels at organization and attention to detail. By working together, you can achieve more than either of you could alone.

6. Strengths and Weaknesses: A Balanced Perspective

While this chapter emphasizes the importance of focusing on your strengths, it's also important to acknowledge your weaknesses. No one is perfect, and we all have areas where we struggle or need improvement. The key is to approach your weaknesses with a balanced perspective.

Instead of being ashamed of your weaknesses, see them as chances to grow or work with others. To succeed, you don't need to be good at everything; you just need to know your strengths and use them well.

Chapter 3

Creating a Vision for Your Future

With a clear understanding of your values and strengths, it's time to look ahead and create a vision for your future. This chapter is about developing a sense of direction and purpose by envisioning the life you truly want to live. While your values and strengths guide you in the present, your vision provides a target to aim for as you navigate the uncertainties and opportunities that lie ahead.

A vision is more than just a set of goals—it's an inspiring and motivating picture of what your ideal future looks like. When you have a clear vision, you can make decisions with more confidence. You also have something to anchor you during times of doubt or challenge. Your vision is a source of inspiration that keeps you on the right track, no matter how winding the path may be.

In this chapter, we'll explore how to create a compelling and authentic vision for your future. We'll also look at how to stay flexible and adaptable while pursuing that vision, allowing it to evolve as you grow.

1. The Power of a Clear Vision

Imagine getting into a car and driving without knowing your destination. You might take some interesting turns, but you're unlikely to end up where you want to be. Life is much the same—if you don't have a clear sense of where you're headed, you risk getting lost, distracted, or pulled off course by external forces.

A clear vision serves as your personal GPS. It helps you stay focused on what truly matters to you and avoid the distractions that can pull you away from your path. It also brings meaning and intention to your actions. When you know what you're working toward, even small, everyday tasks feel more purposeful because they're connected to your larger goals.

More than just providing direction, a vision motivates you. When your vision is rooted in your values and strengths, it's naturally inspiring. It excites you and energizes you, making it easier to stay disciplined and motivated, even when obstacles arise.

2. Envisioning Your Ideal Future

Creating a vision for your future starts with imagining the life you want to live. What would your ideal life look like if you could design it without limits or constraints? This might seem like a daunting question, but the key is to let yourself dream without being restricted by practicalities or fears.

To begin envisioning your future, consider these areas of your life:

- **Career/Work:** What kind of work do you want to be doing? What type of impact do you want to have? What environments and people do you want to surround yourself with?

- **Relationships:** How do you want your relationships to look? This includes family, friends, romantic partners, and your broader community. What kind of connections do you want to cultivate?

- **Personal Growth:** How do you want to evolve as a person? What new skills, experiences, or personal qualities do you want to develop?

- **Health and Well-Being:** What does your ideal state of physical, mental, and emotional health look like? How do you want to feel each day?

- **Lifestyle:** What kind of lifestyle would bring you the most joy and fulfillment? This includes where you live, how you spend your time, and what activities you engage in.

You don't need to have a crystal-clear picture of every detail, but try to get a sense of the direction that feels most aligned with your values, strengths, and desires. What kind of life would give you a sense of purpose and fulfillment?

Exercise: Visualize Your Future

To help clarify your vision, try this simple visualization exercise:

- Find a quiet place where you won't be disturbed. Close your eyes, take a few deep breaths, and relax.

- Imagine yourself five, ten, or even twenty years in the future, living your ideal life. Don't worry about how you got there—just focus on the end result.

- As you visualize this future, pay attention to the details. Where are you? What are you doing? Who are you with? What does your day-to-day life look like? How do you feel?

- Let yourself fully immerse in this future, taking note of the feelings, images, and ideas that arise.

- When you're ready, open your eyes and jot down what you saw and felt during the visualization.

This exercise can help bring your vision to life and give you a clearer sense of where you want to go. Remember, the details don't have to be perfect or precise—the purpose is to capture the essence of what you want your future to feel like.

3. Rooting Your Vision in Your Values

While it's exciting to dream big, it's also essential to ensure that your vision aligns with your core values. If your vision is based solely on external markers of success—like wealth, status, or the expectations of others—it may not lead to true fulfillment, even if you achieve it.

To create a vision that is both inspiring and meaningful, take some time to reflect on how your values fit into your future. Ask yourself:

- **Does my vision reflect what's truly important to me?** For example, if you value creativity, does your vision include opportunities for creative expression? If you value family, does your vision leave room for deep, meaningful connections with loved ones?

- **Am I pursuing this vision for myself, or am I influenced by societal or external pressures?** It's easy to get caught up in what we think we "should" want, but a vision rooted in your authentic values will bring you much more fulfillment than one based on external expectations.

- **How will living this vision help me feel aligned with my values on a daily basis?** Think about how achieving your goals will help you live according to your values.

By ensuring your vision is rooted in your values, you'll be more motivated to pursue it and more likely to experience lasting satisfaction when you achieve it.

4. Balancing Ambition with Flexibility

Creating a compelling vision for your future doesn't mean you need to plan out every detail of your life. In fact, life is unpredictable, and sometimes the best opportunities come from unexpected places. It's important to balance ambition with flexibility, remaining open to new possibilities while staying focused on your broader goals.

Flexibility enables you to adjust and change course when life presents unexpected challenges. It also encourages you to be open to opportunities that may not fit perfectly into your original vision but still align with your values and strengths. Excessive rigidity in pursuing your vision can lead to frustration, particularly when things don't unfold as planned.

Think of your vision as a compass rather than a step-by-step road map. It gives you direction, but it allows for multiple routes to the destination. When new opportunities or challenges arise, ask yourself: Does the situation move me closer to or farther from my vision? If it brings you closer, it may be worth exploring, even if it wasn't part of your original plan.

5. Turning Your Vision into Action

A vision is only powerful if it's followed by action. Once you've envisioned your ideal future, it's time to break that vision down into smaller, actionable steps. This process of translating your vision into concrete actions is what will bring your dreams to life.

Start by asking yourself: What are the major milestones I need to reach to move toward this vision? For example, if your vision includes starting your own business, a milestone might be completing a relevant training program or securing funding. If your vision includes living a healthier lifestyle, a milestone might be developing a consistent exercise routine or adopting healthier eating habits.

From there, break the milestones down into smaller, manageable goals that you can work toward on a daily, weekly, or monthly basis. These smaller goals help you maintain momentum and prevent you from feeling overwhelmed by the bigger picture.

It's important to regularly revisit your vision and your goals, adjusting them as needed. Life is constantly changing, and your vision may evolve. The key is to stay connected to your values and continue taking intentional steps toward the future you want to create.

Exercise: Create a Vision Board

A vision board is a visual representation of your goals, dreams, and aspirations. It can serve as a daily reminder of your vision and help you stay focused on what you're working toward.

To create a vision board:

- Gather materials such as magazines, photos, quotes, or images that inspire you.

- Find a space where you can lay out these materials and start cutting out or printing images that reflect your vision for the future.

- Arrange the images on a board or a piece of paper, organizing them in a way that resonates with you.

- Place your vision board somewhere you'll see it often, like in your office or bedroom. Use it as a source of inspiration and motivation as you work toward your vision.

6. Staying Committed to Your Vision

Achieving a meaningful vision takes time, effort, and persistence. There will be moments of doubt, obstacles, and challenges along the way. During these times, it's essential to stay committed to your vision and trust the process.

One way to maintain your commitment is to regularly reconnect with your "why." Why is this vision important to you? How does it align with your values and strengths? By keeping the deeper purpose behind your vision in mind, you can stay motivated even when the journey becomes difficult.

Another strategy is to celebrate small wins along the way. Every step you take toward your vision—no matter how small—deserves to be acknowledged. Celebrating progress helps build momentum and keeps you motivated to keep going.

Lastly, surround yourself with a supportive network of people who encourage and believe in your vision. Having people who hold you accountable, offer encouragement, and celebrate your successes with you can make all the difference.

Your Vision as a Guidepost

Creating a vision for your future is one of the most powerful tools for staying on the right track in life. Your vision serves as a guidepost, helping you cope with the challenges and opportunities that will inevitably come your way. It gives you a sense of purpose and direction, grounding you in your values and strengths while providing a sense of excitement about what's possible.

Keep in mind, your vision is not static. It can evolve as you grow, learn, and encounter new experiences. The key is to stay true to your goals and values, not to have every detail planned. Your vision is a reflection of your true self and will naturally shift as you gain more clarity about who you are and what brings you fulfillment.

As you continue on this journey, stay open to the unexpected. Life is full of surprises, and sometimes the most meaningful opportunities are the ones you didn't plan for. By staying grounded in your values, leveraging your strengths, and pursuing your vision with flexibility and persistence, you'll be well on your way to living a life that feels purposeful, fulfilling, and aligned with your true self.

In the next chapter, we'll explore how to set goals that align with your vision and values, helping you turn your dreams into reality. You'll learn practical strategies for breaking down your vision into actionable steps and maintaining momentum as you work toward the future you've imagined. Whether you're pursuing personal growth, career success, or deeper relationships, your vision will serve as the foundation for the goals and actions you take moving forward.

Maintain your focus, remain adaptable, and prioritize your vision. You can achieve the future you've imagined by taking small steps, remaining true to yourself, and embracing the journey.

Chapter 4

Setting Goals

Now that you've identified your values, recognized your strengths, and envisioned your ideal future, it's time to get practical. The key to turning your vision into reality is setting clear, actionable goals that align with your values and push you forward on the right track. Goals give you a roadmap for achieving your vision, breaking down your aspirations into manageable steps that can be tracked and adjusted as you progress.

In this chapter, we'll explore the art of goal-setting. You'll learn how to set effective goals that not only move you closer to your vision but also keep you motivated and focused along the way. By the end of this chapter, you'll have the tools you need to create a solid action plan for making your dreams a reality.

1. Why Goal-Setting Matters

Goals are powerful because they transform your vision into something tangible. Without goals, your vision remains an abstract idea—a distant dream that feels difficult to reach. Setting goals provides a structure for turning that dream into reality by giving you a clear direction, deadlines, and milestones to work toward.

Goals also help you stay motivated. When you have specific objectives to work toward, each small victory provides a sense of accomplishment, which fuels your desire to keep going. Conversely, without concrete goals, it's easy to feel overwhelmed by the enormity of your vision or unsure of where to start. Goals bring clarity and focus, helping you prioritize your actions and stay on track.

2. The SMART Goal Framework

One of the most effective ways to set meaningful and achievable goals is by using the SMART goal framework. SMART stands for Specific, Measurable, Achievable, Relevant, and Time-bound. This framework ensures that your goals are clear, realistic, and actionable, giving you a higher chance of success.

Let's break down each component of the SMART framework:

- **Specific:** A specific goal is clear and well-defined. It answers the question: What do you want to achieve? Why is this goal important? Who is involved? Where will it take place? For example, instead of setting a vague goal like "get fit," a specific goal would be "run a 5K race in three months."

- **Measurable:** A measurable goal has concrete criteria for tracking your progress. This helps you stay motivated and know when you've reached your goal. For example, a measurable goal related to fitness could be "run three miles without stopping" or "lose 10 pounds in two months." Measuring your progress allows you to adjust your efforts as needed.

- **Achievable:** Your goal should be realistic and attainable based on your current situation and resources. While it's important to challenge yourself, setting goals that are too ambitious can lead to frustration and burnout. Make sure your goal is within reach but requires effort and growth.

- **Relevant:** A relevant goal is aligned with your larger vision and values. Ask yourself: Does this goal move me closer to my vision? Is it aligned with my long-term objectives? For example, if your vision is to live a healthier lifestyle, a goal to run a 5K might be relevant, while a goal to learn to play the piano may not be as closely tied to your current focus.

- **Time-bound:** A time-bound goal has a specific deadline or timeframe for completion. This creates a sense of urgency and helps you stay accountable. For example, instead of saying, "I want to run a 5K someday," a time-bound goal would be, "I want to run a 5K by June 30th."

By using the SMART framework, you can ensure that your goals are clear, realistic, and aligned with your overall vision.

3. Breaking Down Long-Term Goals

It's important to have both long-term and short-term goals. Typically, long-term goals align with your larger vision and can take months or even years to achieve. For example, completing a degree, starting a business, or saving for a down payment on a house could be long-term goals.

However, long-term goals can often feel overwhelming if you don't break them down into smaller, more manageable steps. This is where short-term goals come into play. Short-term goals help you stay focused and make steady progress toward your larger objectives. They create a sense of momentum, allowing you to celebrate small wins along the way.

For example, if your long-term goal is to start your own business in two years, you could break it down into smaller goals like:

- **Month 1:** Research your industry and identify a business niche.

- **Month 2:** Develop a business plan and identify potential funding sources.

- **Month 3:** Set up your website and branding materials.

- **Month 4:** Begin networking and marketing to potential clients.

By breaking down your long-term goals into smaller, more achievable milestones, you'll be able to maintain motivation and track your progress over time.

4. The Power of Accountability

Accountability plays a key role in achieving your goals. When you share your goals with others or set up systems of accountability, you're more likely to stay committed and follow through. Knowing that someone else is keeping track of your progress can provide extra motivation, especially when you face obstacles or feel tempted to give up.

Here are a few ways to create accountability for your goals:

- **Share Your Goals:** Tell a friend, family member, or mentor about your goals and ask them to check in on your progress regularly. The simple act of sharing your goals with someone else increases your commitment to achieving them.

- **Join a Group or Community:** Joining a group or community of like-minded individuals who are working toward similar goals can be incredibly motivating. Whether it's a fitness group, a mastermind group for entrepreneurs, or an online community focused on personal growth, surrounding yourself with people who share your ambitions can help keep you accountable. You can share your successes, seek advice when you face challenges, and find inspiration in the progress of others.

- **Hire a Coach or Mentor:** If you're serious about staying on track, consider hiring a coach or mentor who can provide guidance, feedback, and support. A coach can help you clarify your goals, develop a plan of action, and hold you accountable for meeting your deadlines. A mentor can offer valuable insights based on their own experience and keep you grounded when you're feeling unsure or overwhelmed.

- **Use Tracking Tools:** Whether it's a simple notebook, a goal-setting app, or a project management tool, tracking your progress is another effective way to hold yourself accountable. By keeping a record of your goals and the steps you're taking toward achieving them, you create a tangible reminder of your commitment. Reviewing your progress regularly helps you stay focused and adjust your approach if needed.

5. Overcoming Obstacles and Staying Flexible

Even the most meticulous plans face challenges. As you work toward your goals, there will be times when things don't go as expected, when you feel discouraged, or when obstacles seem insurmountable. The key to overcoming these challenges is resilience and flexibility.

Here are some strategies to help you overcome obstacles and keep moving forward:

- **Anticipate Roadblocks:** Before you start working toward a goal, take some time to anticipate potential challenges. What obstacles might you encounter along the way? Whether it's time constraints, lack of resources, or unexpected life events, identifying potential roadblocks in advance allows you to prepare mentally and come up with contingency plans. This will ensure that you are prepared for any challenges that may arise.

- **Be Kind to Yourself:** No one's journey is perfect. There will be setbacks, and you may experience moments of self-doubt or frustration. When these moments occur, it's important to practice self-compassion. Instead of criticizing yourself for not meeting a deadline or struggling with a particular challenge, acknowledge that growth takes time. Celebrate your efforts, and remind yourself that progress is not always linear.

- **Stay Flexible:** While it's important to have a clear vision and specific goals, life is unpredictable. As you work toward your goals, remain open to adjusting your plan. Flexibility allows you to pivot when necessary without losing sight of your overarching vision. If one path doesn't work out, there are often alternative routes to your destination.

- **Reframe Setbacks as Learning Opportunities:** When obstacles arise, it's easy to view them as failures. However, setbacks are often valuable learning opportunities. Each challenge you encounter is a chance to learn more about yourself, improve your strategies, and build resilience. Ask yourself: What can I learn from this experience? How can I adjust my approach moving forward?

6. Celebrating Progress and Small Wins

It's common to become so engrossed in achieving your larger goals that you neglect to acknowledge and celebrate the smaller milestones along the journey. However, acknowledging and celebrating your progress is essential for maintaining motivation and reinforcing positive behaviors. Each step you take, no matter how small, brings you closer to your vision, and it's important to recognize those achievements.

Here are some ways to celebrate your progress:

- **Track Your Achievements:** As you work toward your goals, keep a record of your achievements. Whether it's completing a small task, reaching a milestone, or overcoming an obstacle, write down your successes. Reviewing your accomplishments can provide a powerful reminder of how far you've come.

- **Reward Yourself:** Set up a system of rewards for achieving specific milestones. These rewards can be small—such as treating yourself to a delicious meal, taking a break to relax, or indulging in a favorite activity. Knowing there's a reward waiting for you can make the process more enjoyable and keep you motivated.

- **Reflect on Your Growth:** Take time to reflect on how far you've grown since you began working toward your goals. Have you developed new skills? Gained confidence? Have you gained a greater appreciation for yourself or your vision? By focusing on your personal growth, you'll reinforce the belief that progress isn't just about achieving the end goal—it's about the journey and the lessons you learn along the way.

7. Revisiting and Adjusting Your Goals

Your goals are not static. As you grow and evolve, your priorities, circumstances, and vision may change. Periodically reviewing your goals is crucial to confirm their alignment with your values and future vision. Don't be afraid to adjust your goals if necessary—whether that means shifting your focus, extending your timeline, or setting entirely new goals.

Here's how to stay adaptable and responsive to changes:

- **Regularly Review Your Goals:** Consider scheduling regular check-ins with yourself to evaluate your progress and confirm that your goals remain relevant. You might do these activities once a month or once every quarter, depending on the complexity of your goals. Ask yourself: Am I still passionate about this goal? Does it still align with my vision and values? What adjustments, if any, do I need to make?

- **Be Honest with Yourself:** It's okay to change direction if a goal no longer resonates with you. Sometimes, as we pursue a goal, we realize it's not what we truly want. Rather than pushing forward out of obligation, be honest with yourself about whether the goal is still worth pursuing. If not, kindly allow yourself the flexibility to pivot.

- **Celebrate Growth, Not Just Achievements:** Sometimes, even if you don't reach your original goal, the growth and experience you gain along the way are just as valuable. Concentrate on what you've learned, how you've improved, and how to apply those lessons to your next goals.

From Vision to Reality

Setting clear, actionable goals is a crucial step in turning your vision for the future into reality. By using the SMART goal framework, breaking down long-term goals into manageable steps, and holding yourself accountable, you'll create a roadmap that guides you toward your dreams.

Remember that the journey toward your goals will not always be smooth, but with resilience, flexibility, and a focus on celebrating progress, you'll be able to navigate the obstacles and challenges that arise. Your goals are not just a checklist of tasks—they're a reflection of your values, strengths, and vision for the life you want to live.

In the next chapter, we'll explore the inevitable obstacles and setbacks you may encounter along the way and provide strategies for overcoming them with confidence and determination. You'll learn how to stay resilient in the face of challenges and continue moving forward, even when the path seems difficult. With a strong foundation of goals, values, and vision, you'll be well-prepared to tackle whatever comes your way.

Chapter 5

Overcoming Obstacles

No matter how well-prepared or focused you are, obstacles are an inevitable part of any journey. Whether they come in the form of external challenges, internal struggles, or unexpected circumstances, obstacles can slow you down, cause frustration, and sometimes make you question whether you're on the right track. However, how you confront and overcome obstacles can significantly impact your ability to achieve your goals and remain true to your vision.

In this chapter, we will explore strategies for overcoming obstacles with resilience and determination. You'll learn how to reframe challenges, build mental toughness, and develop practical approaches to keep moving forward when things get tough. By the end of this chapter, you will possess the necessary tools and mindset to navigate the inevitable roadblocks and stay on course towards the life you envision.

1. Understanding the Nature of Obstacles

Before we dive into strategies for overcoming obstacles, it's important to recognize that they are a natural part of any journey toward growth and achievement. No one reaches their goals without encountering challenges along the way. Obstacles, whether big or small, are opportunities for learning, adaptation, and strengthening your resolve.

Obstacles come in many forms:

- **External obstacles** are challenges that arise from outside circumstances, such as lack of resources, time constraints, financial limitations, or societal expectations. These are often things you have little to no control over but must navigate nonetheless.

- **Internal obstacles** are challenges that arise from within, such as self-doubt, fear of failure, procrastination, or limiting beliefs. These are often the most difficult obstacles to overcome because they require you to confront your own mindset and emotions.

- **Unexpected events** can also disrupt your plans, such as sudden changes in your personal life, health challenges, or global events (like a pandemic). While these events are beyond your control, how you respond to them will determine whether you're able to stay on track.

Recognizing the type of obstacle you're facing can help you choose the best strategy for overcoming it. The key is to approach each challenge with a mindset of resilience and adaptability, viewing obstacles not as roadblocks but as opportunities to grow stronger and more resourceful.

2. Reframing Obstacles as Opportunities

One of the most powerful strategies for overcoming obstacles is to reframe them as opportunities. While challenges can feel discouraging or frustrating in the moment, they often provide valuable lessons and opportunities for growth that you wouldn't have encountered otherwise.

Consider these ways to reframe obstacles:

- **Obstacles build resilience.** Every time you face a challenge and work through it, you become more resilient. You develop the ability to handle adversity, think creatively, and adapt to changing circumstances. The next time you encounter a similar obstacle, you'll be better equipped to handle it with confidence.

- **Obstacles offer a chance for learning.** Obstacles often reveal gaps in your knowledge, skills, or resources. Instead of viewing these gaps as setbacks, see them as opportunities to learn and grow. What can you learn from this obstacle that will make you stronger or more prepared in the future?

- **Obstacles help you clarify your goals.** Sometimes, encountering an obstacle forces you to reevaluate your goals and determine whether they are truly aligned with your values and vision. An obstacle may cause you to pivot, refine your approach, or adjust your goals in a way that brings you closer to your authentic self.

Reframing obstacles in this way allows you to approach them with curiosity rather than frustration. When you view challenges as opportunities, you're more likely to embrace them with a positive attitude and creative problem-solving mindset.

3. Developing a Resilient Mindset

A resilient mindset is crucial for overcoming obstacles and staying on the right track. Resilience is the ability to bounce back from setbacks, adapt to difficult situations, and maintain a sense of optimism even when things don't go as planned.

Here are some key components of a resilient mindset:

- **Embrace failure as part of the process.** Failure is not the opposite of success—it's part of the journey toward success. When you view failure as a learning opportunity rather than a personal shortcoming, you're more likely to take risks and persevere through difficulties. Instead of avoiding failure, embrace it as a stepping stone to growth.

- **Practice gratitude in difficult times.** Gratitude shifts your focus from what's going wrong to what's going right. Even in the face of obstacles, there's always something to be grateful for, whether it's the support of loved ones, the lessons you're learning, or the progress you've already made. Practicing gratitude helps you maintain perspective and resilience during tough times.

- **Stay flexible and adaptable.** Life rarely goes exactly as planned, and the ability to adapt to changing circumstances is key to overcoming obstacles. A rigid mindset can leave you feeling stuck when things don't go as expected, while a flexible mindset allows you to pivot and adjust your approach. Remember that there's often more than one way to reach your goals.

- **Focus on what you can control.** When facing obstacles, it's easy to become overwhelmed by things that are outside of your control. Instead of dwelling on what you can't change, focus on what you can control—your actions, your mindset, and your response to the challenge. By directing your energy toward things within your control, you'll feel more empowered and capable of overcoming the obstacle.

4. Strategies for Overcoming Obstacles

In addition to developing a resilient mindset, there are several practical strategies you can use to overcome obstacles and stay moving forward:

- **Break the Obstacle Down.** When you're faced with a big challenge, it can feel overwhelming. One way to overcome this feeling is to break the obstacle down into smaller, more manageable parts. Ask yourself: What is the first step I can take to address this challenge? Focusing on one small step at a time allows you to gradually overcome the obstacle and make progress. For example, if you're struggling to complete a large project, break it down into smaller tasks and tackle them one at a time. Each small victory will give you the momentum you need to keep going.

- **Seek Support.** You don't have to face obstacles alone. One of the most effective ways to overcome challenges is to seek support from others. Whether it's a mentor, a friend, a colleague, or a coach, having someone to provide guidance, encouragement, and a fresh perspective can make a significant difference. Don't be afraid to ask for help when you need it. Sometimes, an outside perspective can help you see solutions that you might not have considered on your own.

- **Revisit Your "Why."** When obstacles arise, it's easy to lose sight of why you started your journey in the first place. Reconnecting with your "why"—the deeper reason behind your goals and vision—can provide the motivation you need to push through challenges. Ask yourself: Why is this goal important to me? How does it align with my values and vision for the future? Reminding yourself of the purpose behind your actions can reignite your passion and help you stay focused, even in the face of difficulty.

- **Adjust Your Approach.** If you've been working on a goal and continuously encountering obstacles, it might be time to adjust your approach. Instead of giving up, consider whether there's a different way to tackle the challenge. Could you try a new strategy, seek additional resources, or break the goal into smaller steps? Occasionally, a small adjustment is all it takes to overcome an obstacle and move forward. Stay open to experimentation and be willing to pivot when necessary.

5. Building Long-Term Resilience

Overcoming obstacles isn't just about getting through a single challenge—it's about building long-term resilience that will help you navigate the ups and downs of life with strength and grace.

Here are some ways to build long-term resilience:

- **Develop healthy coping mechanisms.** When faced with stress or setbacks, it's important to have healthy ways to cope. Whether it's exercise, meditation, journaling, or spending time with loved ones, having go-to coping mechanisms can help you manage stress and maintain your mental well-being.

- **Focus on progress, not perfection.** Perfectionism can be a major obstacle in itself. Instead of striving for perfection, focus on making progress. Each small step forward is a victory, even if the journey is imperfect. By celebrating progress, you'll build confidence and resilience over time.

- **Cultivate a growth mindset.** The belief in developing your abilities and intelligence through effort and learning is known as a growth mindset. People with a growth mindset see challenges as opportunities to grow, rather than as threats to their self-worth. By adopting a growth mindset, you'll be more willing to take risks, learn from failure, and embrace the process of growth.

- **Build a strong support network.** Surround yourself with people who encourage you, believe in you, and support your goals. A strong support network provides a safety net during difficult times, offering advice, empathy, and encouragement when you need it most.

Embracing the Journey

Obstacles are an inevitable part of any meaningful journey, but they don't have to derail your progress. By reframing challenges as opportunities, developing a resilient mindset, and using practical strategies to overcome obstacles, you can stay on track and continue moving toward your vision.

Remember, overcoming obstacles is not about avoiding challenges altogether—it's about embracing the journey, learning from setbacks, and growing stronger with each step. The obstacles you face are not roadblocks; they are stepping stones that help you become more resourceful, determined, and aligned with your purpose.

As you continue on your path, trust in your ability to overcome whatever challenges come your way. Stay focused on your vision, lean on your strengths, and approach obstacles with confidence and resilience.

In the next chapter, we'll explore how to adjust your course when life's circumstances change or when your goals evolve, ensuring that you remain flexible and adaptable on your journey. Life is full of unexpected turns, and learning how to adjust your course without losing sight of your overall vision is a crucial skill for staying on the right track.

As we move forward, you'll learn how to assess your progress, make necessary changes, and stay connected to your values even when the path ahead looks different than you originally planned.

Chapter 6

Adjusting Your Course

As you pursue your goals and work toward the vision you've set for yourself, life may throw unexpected changes your way. Whether it's a shift in your career, a change in your personal life, or new challenges that arise, being flexible and willing to adjust your course is key to staying on track. Sometimes, the direction you thought was right for you no longer serves your values or brings you fulfillment. Other times, circumstances beyond your control force you to rethink your approach.

This chapter is about learning how to adapt and pivot when necessary without losing sight of your overall vision. Adjusting your course doesn't mean giving up on your dreams—it means finding new ways to achieve them and being open to the growth that comes from change.

1. Recognizing When It's Time to Adjust

One of the most important skills in navigating life's journey is recognizing when it's time to adjust your course. It can be tempting to stick to a plan simply because you've invested time and effort into it, but clinging too tightly to a rigid path can lead to frustration and burnout.

Here are some signs that it may be time to adjust your course:

- **Loss of Passion:** If you no longer feel excited or motivated by your goals, it may be a sign that your values or interests have shifted. It's natural for your passions to evolve, and it's important to be honest with yourself about whether your current path still aligns with who you are.

- **Constant Setbacks:** While obstacles are a normal part of any journey, if you find yourself facing repeated setbacks that feel insurmountable, it may be worth reassessing your approach. Are you pursuing a goal that no longer feels realistic or aligned with your strengths? Are there alternative routes that could lead to the same destination?

- **Changing Circumstances:** Life is unpredictable, and external circumstances—such as health issues, family responsibilities, or economic changes—can impact your ability to pursue your goals in the way you originally intended. When life changes, it's important to reassess your priorities and find ways to adapt.

- **New Opportunities:** Sometimes, adjusting your course isn't about reacting to setbacks but about seizing new opportunities. If a new path presents itself that excites you or feels more aligned with your values, don't be afraid to explore it, even if it means changing direction.

2. Embracing Change as a Natural Part of the Journey

Change is a constant in life, and learning to embrace it rather than resist it is crucial for long-term success and fulfillment. Instead of viewing change as a disruption, try to see it as an opportunity for growth and self-discovery.

Here are some ways to embrace change:

- **Stay Open-Minded:** Be open to the possibility that your original plan may not be the only path to achieving your vision. Life often presents unexpected opportunities that, while initially outside of your plan, may offer new ways to grow and achieve your goals. Keeping an open mind allows you to explore these opportunities without feeling constrained by your original plan.

- **Reframe Change as Growth:** Every change, whether positive or negative, brings with it the opportunity to learn and grow. Instead of focusing on what you're losing or what's uncertain, focus on the new possibilities that change brings. What can you learn from this shift? How can you use this experience to become more resilient, adaptable, and aligned with your true self?

- **Trust the Process:** Even when change feels uncomfortable, trust that it's part of your journey. Life rarely unfolds exactly as we expect, and sometimes the greatest opportunities for growth come from the most unexpected places. By trusting the process and staying open to change, you can navigate uncertainty with confidence.

3. How to Adjust Your Course Without Losing Sight of Your Vision

Adjusting your course doesn't mean abandoning your vision. It's about finding new ways to stay aligned with your values and purpose, even when the path ahead looks different than you originally imagined.

Here's how to adjust your course while staying true to your vision:

- **Revisit Your Values:** When circumstances change, revisit your core values to ensure that any adjustments you make are aligned with what matters most to you. Your values act as a compass, guiding you through uncertainty and helping you make decisions that feel authentic and meaningful. Ask yourself: How can I stay true to my values as I navigate this change?

- **Set New Goals:** Once you've reassessed your values and determined the best way to adjust your course, set new, realistic goals that reflect your current situation. These goals may look different from your original ones, but as long as they align with your vision and values, they will keep you moving forward.

- **Maintain Focus on the Bigger Picture:** Despite the potential changes in the details of your journey, remain mindful of the broader picture. Your overall vision—whether it's to live a more fulfilling life, make a positive impact, or achieve personal growth—remains your guiding light. Even if the specific steps you take change, your vision will keep you grounded and motivated.

- **Let Go of Perfectionism:** When adjusting your course, it's important to let go of the idea that there's a "perfect" way to achieve your goals. Life is full of complexities, and every journey is filled with unexpected challenges. By releasing the need for perfection, you'll be more open to adapting and finding new ways to stay on track.

4. Practical Steps for Pivoting in a New Direction

If you've decided it's time to adjust your course, here are some practical steps you can take to pivot in a new direction:

- **Assess Your Current Situation:** Take stock of where you are right now. What's working, and what's not? What has changed in your life, and how does that impact your goals? This honest assessment will give you a clear picture of where you need to make adjustments.

- **Identify New Opportunities:** Search for new opportunities that align with your values and vision. These could be new career paths, creative projects, personal development opportunities, or even lifestyle changes. Be open to exploring options that you may not have considered before.

- **Create a Flexible Action Plan:** Once you've identified a new direction, create an action plan that outlines the steps you need to take. However, keep the plan flexible. Life is dynamic, and being willing to adjust your plan as you go will allow you to stay resilient and adaptable.

- **Seek Guidance and Support:** If you're feeling unsure about how to adjust your course, seek guidance from trusted mentors, coaches, or friends. Sometimes, an outside perspective can offer valuable insights and help you gain clarity on the best path forward.

5. Celebrating Your Evolution

Adjusting your course is not a sign of failure—it's a sign of growth. As you navigate changes and challenges, celebrate the evolution of your journey. Every adjustment you make is an opportunity to become more aligned with your authentic self and your true purpose.

Recognize that your journey is unique to you, and there's no "right" way to achieve your goals. Staying open, flexible, and true to your values will bring you closer to the life you desire.

Navigating Life's Changes with Confidence

Adaptability and alignment with your values enable you to confidently navigate the inevitable changes in life. Adjusting your course doesn't mean abandoning your vision—it means finding new ways to stay true to yourself and your goals, even when the path looks different than you originally planned.

In the final chapter, we'll explore how to measure success and redefine progress in a way that reflects your unique journey. You'll learn how to stay fulfilled by focusing on personal growth, alignment with your values, and the joy of the journey itself.

Chapter 7

Embracing Change and Uncertainty

In our quest to be on the "right track," we often long for clarity and certainty. We want to know that the steps we're taking will lead us exactly where we want to go. However, life is rarely that predictable. Adapting to change is vital to staying on track, as uncertainty is unavoidable.

This chapter explores the importance of embracing change, uncertainty, and the unexpected twists that life throws your way. While it's natural to resist uncertainty, it's often in these moments that we experience the greatest growth and transformation. Acknowledging and managing change not only helps you stay on course, but it can also lead to unanticipated opportunities.

1. The Nature of Change: Why It's Inevitable

One of the first truths we must accept is that change is inevitable. No matter how well we plan or how carefully we map out our future, life is dynamic. Situations shift, people change, and external factors beyond our control come into play. Learn to recognize the different types of change—whether they are planned, unexpected, or gradual—and how each one can impact your path.

2. Reframing Your Mindset: Viewing Change as Growth

Many people fear change because it introduces uncertainty and discomfort. However, what if you reframed change as an opportunity for growth and learning? Explore practical strategies to rewire your mindset so that you see change not as a disruption but as a powerful tool for personal and professional development. The more flexible you become, the easier it will be to stay on the right track, even when that track evolves over time.

3. Building Emotional Resilience

Adapting to change isn't just about strategic thinking—it's also an emotional challenge. When faced with major life shifts, it's common to experience anxiety, stress, or even grief over what's being left behind. Focus on emotional resilience and how to build it. Through techniques such as mindfulness, journaling, and self-compassion, you'll learn how to manage your emotions effectively during periods of uncertainty and change.

4. Letting Go of Perfectionism

Perfectionism can keep us stuck. When we hold on too tightly to a specific vision of what life should look like, we become rigid and resistant to the natural flow of events. Recognize the dangers of perfectionism and realize how letting go of rigid expectations can free you to explore new paths and possibilities. Remember, being on the right track doesn't mean everything is perfect—it means you're moving in a direction aligned with your core values and goals.

5. The Power of Small, Flexible Goals

When navigating a period of change or uncertainty, it's important to revisit your goals. Large, long-term goals can sometimes feel daunting in the face of change, making it difficult to take any action at all. Recognize the significance of establishing small, adaptable objectives that you can modify as necessary. Learn how to create milestones that keep you moving forward without feeling overwhelmed by the unknown.

6. Learning to Trust Yourself and the Process

One of the most difficult parts of embracing uncertainty is learning to trust yourself and the process of life. In moments of change, it's easy to doubt your abilities or feel lost.

Use the techniques suggested in this book for building self-trust through daily habits, affirmations, and taking calculated risks. Trust that the process of life will unfold in its own time, often in ways you couldn't predict but that serve your long-term growth.

7. Practical Tools for Navigating Major Life Transitions

Whether it's a career change, a relationship shift, or a relocation to a new city, major life transitions require practical strategies. Discover different tools for making smart decisions when facing significant changes, including how to gather information, assess risks, and make choices aligned with your values. Learn the importance of cultivating a support system to help you through times of transition.

8. Finding Opportunity in Setbacks

Sometimes change doesn't come in the form of an exciting new opportunity—it comes as a setback or disappointment. Perhaps you didn't get the job you wanted, or a business venture didn't go as planned. Learn how to find opportunity even in failure. You will also learn to see setbacks as stepping stones that lead you to your true path.

Change and uncertainty are not detours off the right track—they are part of the track itself. Embracing them can lead to growth, new opportunities, and a deeper understanding of yourself. By cultivating flexibility, resilience, and a mindset of possibility, you can stay on course, even when the course changes. Remember, life is not a straight path but a winding journey, and every turn has the potential to lead you to something extraordinary.

Accepting change enables you to relish the process of discovery, which is the essence of staying on the right path.

Chapter 8

Measuring Success and Redefining Progress

We often associate being on the "right track" with traditional markers of success, such as career advancement, financial wealth, or societal recognition. But what if the path to fulfillment doesn't align with these external definitions of success?

In this chapter, we explore how to measure success in a way that is personally meaningful and how to redefine progress on your journey.

True success is a deeply personal concept, deeply rooted in your individual values, aspirations, and life circumstances. We will look beyond conventional success metrics and provide tools to help you define and measure success on your own terms.

1. Challenging Traditional Definitions of Success

Society often defines success as a prestigious job, a certain income level, or a checklist of achievements. While these markers can be part of success, they may not lead to true happiness or fulfillment. Sometimes you need to challenge the conventional ideas of success and ask yourself what it means to you personally. Is it about impact? Is it about balance and quality of life? Or is it about continuous learning and growth?

Explore examples of individuals who have chosen unconventional paths—people who have turned down high-paying jobs to pursue passions, who have redefined what "winning" means, and who have discovered success through service or creativity. The aim is to broaden your understanding of success beyond societal pressures and expectations.

2. Defining Success Based on Your Values

One of the key insights mentioned earlier is that aligning with your core values is essential to finding the right track. Dive deeper into how you can measure success by aligning your progress with your values. Engage in exercises to identify what truly matters to you and how you can create metrics for success that reflect those priorities.

For example, if family and relationships are your highest value, success might look like creating a life where you have ample time and energy to nurture those relationships. If personal growth is your primary value, you may measure success by how much you've learned or how many new experiences you've had. The goal is to redefine success in ways that align with your authentic self.

3. Recognizing Non-Linear Progress

Progress is often thought of as a straight line—steady, upward movement toward a goal. However, real-life progress is rarely linear. There are setbacks, plateaus, and sometimes even periods of regression. Nevertheless, you need to recognize and appreciate progress, even when it doesn't follow a linear path.

Read and appreciate stories of individuals who experienced long periods of stagnation before breakthroughs or who took what seemed like detours but ultimately led them to where they needed to be. Learn how to reframe these periods of uncertainty or seeming lack of progress as valuable experiences that contribute to your overall growth.

4. The Role of Personal Fulfillment in Measuring Success

While external achievements are important, personal fulfillment is perhaps the most accurate indicator of whether you are on the right track. Discover the often overlooked internal markers of success, such as joy, contentment, a sense of purpose, and emotional well-being. These intangible qualities hold equal, if not greater, significance than external measures of success.

Use practical techniques for tracking your personal fulfillment, such as journaling about what brings you joy, reflecting on moments when you feel most at peace, and assessing whether you feel a sense of meaning in your daily activities.

5. The Danger of Comparison

Comparing your journey to others is one of the biggest obstacles to staying on track. In the age of social media, it's easy to look at someone else's life and feel inadequate, as though their success highlights your perceived failures. Be aware of the dangers of comparison, and learn how to avoid falling into the trap of measuring yourself against others.

Remember to use different techniques for practicing gratitude and self-compassion, and recognize the importance of focusing on your unique journey. By letting go of the need to compare, you can focus on your own progress and find joy in your personal path.

6. Small Wins and Micro-Successes: The Power of Incremental Progress

Success doesn't always have to be about large milestones. Sometimes, the small wins and micro-successes along the way are just as significant. Discover the hidden power of incremental progress and learn how to recognize and celebrate the small victories that contribute to your overall success.

Whether it's mastering a new skill, overcoming a personal fear, or taking a step outside your comfort zone, these small moments of achievement can serve as powerful motivators. Learn how to cultivate a mindset that celebrates small wins that can build momentum and keep you moving forward on your journey.

7. Redefining Failure: A Tool for Growth

Many people fear failure because it's seen as the opposite of success. However, failure can be redefined as a tool for growth rather than a setback. So-called failures are often considered essential learning opportunities that lead to greater success in the long run.

Read stories of successful people who failed multiple times before achieving their goals, and you'll learn how to develop a mindset that views failure as an integral part of the journey. Reframing failure allows you to maintain focus even when unexpected events occur.

8. Creating Your Own Success Roadmap

It's time to create your own personal roadmap for success. This isn't just about setting goals—it's about identifying how you will measure progress in meaningful ways, aligned with your values and aspirations.

Practice exercises to help you set intentional success markers, both big and small, and then you'll learn how to regularly evaluate your progress based on personal fulfillment, growth, and happiness. The aim is to create a dynamic and flexible success roadmap that evolves with you over time.

Success is not a destination; it's an ongoing journey. The more you learn to define success on your own terms, the more empowered you'll feel to stay on the right track, even when life's path winds unexpectedly. By aligning your goals with your values, recognizing both big and small progress, and avoiding the pitfalls of comparison, you can live a life that feels fulfilling and meaningful.

Remember, true success is deeply personal. It's about living authentically, growing continuously, and finding joy in the process. When you redefine success in these terms, you'll find that the right track isn't a fixed path—it's a journey of discovery, adaptation, and fulfillment that evolves with you.

Chapter 9

Building a Support System for Your Journey

No matter how strong, resilient, or self-sufficient we are, no one can go through life alone. One of the most important elements for staying on the right track is to surround yourself with a supportive network of people who uplift, challenge, and guide you when you need it most. In this chapter, we'll explore the importance of building and maintaining a solid support system that aligns with your values and vision.

As you work toward your goals and navigate life's changes, the people around you can either be your greatest asset or a significant source of distraction and doubt. The key is to consciously cultivate a community that helps you grow, while also knowing how to give back and contribute meaningfully to the lives of others.

1. The Power of Connection: Why a Support System is Essential

Human beings are wired for connection. Having a supportive community around you can make a significant difference, whether you're working toward a major goal, facing challenges, or simply trying to stay on the right track in life. Successful people attest to the psychological and emotional benefits of having a strong support system, including reduced stress, increased motivation, and improved problem-solving abilities.

Learn how different types of relationships—personal, professional, and community-based—can contribute to your overall well-being and progress. From close friendships to mentorship relationships, a diverse support system will provide you with the resources and encouragement you need to thrive.

2. Identifying the Right People: Quality Over Quantity

When it comes to building your support system, it's not about having the largest network—it's about having the *right* people in your corner. Learn how to identify the qualities you should look for in the individuals who make up your support network. Some people will challenge you to grow, others will provide a safe space for you to be vulnerable, and still others will offer expert advice or mentorship. Dr. Napoleon Hill, in his best-selling book, *"Think and Grow Rich,"* calls it your *"Mastermind Alliance."*

Learn how to evaluate your current relationships and determine which ones align with your values, goals, and emotional needs. Learn how to set boundaries with people who may drain your energy or steer you off track, while also fostering deeper connections with those who inspire and uplift you.

3. Building Mutually Supportive Relationships

Support systems are not one-sided; they are built on mutual respect, trust, and reciprocity. Discover how to establish relationships that are both balanced and mutually beneficial. Whether it's friendships, romantic partnerships, or professional collaborations, every strong relationship is based on giving as well as receiving.

Remember to show up for the people in your life, provide emotional and practical support when needed, and cultivate relationships that thrive on mutual growth. By building mutually supportive connections, you'll create a network that's based on trust, care, and shared values.

4. Finding Mentors and Role Models

In addition to friends and family, mentors and role models play a crucial role in helping you stay on the right track. These are individuals who have experience in areas you aspire to grow in and who can offer valuable guidance and perspective.

Take the time to go through the process of finding and approaching potential mentors, whether in your career, personal life, or creative pursuits. Learn how to build genuine relationships with mentors, how to seek advice without overburdening them, and how to apply their insights to your own life. Additionally, explore how role models—people you admire but may not personally know—can inspire and influence your journey.

5. Asking for Help: Overcoming the Fear of Vulnerability

Many people struggle with asking for help, viewing it as a sign of weakness or fearing rejection. However, asking for support is a crucial aspect of building and maintaining strong relationships. Understand why vulnerability is a strength and how opening up to others can deepen your connections and provide the support you need to move forward.

Learn practical tips for asking for help in a way that feels comfortable, including how to express your needs and how to choose the right moments to seek support. Be open to receiving help without feeling guilty or indebted.

6. Cultivating a Positive Environment

Your support system doesn't just consist of people—it's also about the environments you immerse yourself in. Focus on creating positive, nurturing spaces that foster growth, creativity, and well-being. Whether it's your physical environment (home, workspace, or social spaces) or your mental and emotional atmosphere, you have the power to shape your surroundings to support your journey.

Learn how to build environments that encourage focus and positivity, as well as how to distance yourself from toxic influences that hinder your progress. This might mean curating a healthier social media feed, finding communities that share your interests and values, or creating a living space that inspires you.

7. Networking with Intention: Building Professional Connections

In today's interconnected world, professional networking is an essential part of staying on the right track, especially in your career or business pursuits. However, networking isn't just about collecting business cards or making superficial connections—it's about building meaningful relationships that can lead to collaboration, mentorship, and shared growth.

Discover strategies for networking with intention. Learn how to approach networking events, online communities, and professional circles with authenticity, how to nurture long-term professional relationships, and how to find opportunities for mutual benefit. By connecting with the right people in your field, you can open doors to new opportunities while offering your skills and insights in return.

8. The Importance of Giving Back

No support system is complete without the element of giving back. Understand the importance of contributing to the well-being of others. Whether through mentoring, volunteering, or simply being a good friend, giving back strengthens your relationships and reinforces your sense of purpose.

Endeavor to identify ways you can offer support to others, whether that's through acts of kindness, sharing resources, or offering emotional support. Giving back is not only an essential part of maintaining healthy relationships, but it also reinforces your role within your community and keeps you connected to a larger purpose.

Building and maintaining a support system is one of the most important factors in staying on the right track in life. While personal drive and ambition are essential, it's the people around you who provide the encouragement, advice, and accountability needed to reach your goals. By surrounding yourself with the right individuals, cultivating mutually supportive relationships, and knowing when to ask for help, you can create a network that empowers you to keep moving forward, even when the road gets tough.

Support systems are about giving and receiving help. By fostering meaningful connections, both personally and professionally, you create a web of support that enriches not only your own journey but also the journeys of those around you. This interconnectedness is one of the most powerful tools for staying aligned with your values and achieving lasting success.

Chapter 10

Staying Aligned with Your True Self

As we conclude this journey of exploring whether you're on the right track, it's important to point out that the ultimate destination is not a specific achievement or external validation, but rather the ongoing practice of staying aligned with your true self. While goals and circumstances may change over time, the foundation of living a fulfilling and meaningful life is your ability to remain connected to your authentic self—the person you are at your core, beneath the layers of societal expectations, external pressures, and fears.

In this final chapter, we will explore the practices, mindsets, and habits that will help you maintain that alignment with your true self, regardless of what challenges or opportunities life presents. The process of self-alignment is not static; it requires constant reflection, adjustment, and growth. This chapter aims to help you grow while remaining authentic.

1. The Importance of Authenticity

Living authentically means embracing your unique strengths, values, and desires, rather than conforming to others' expectations. Understand that authenticity is crucial for long-term fulfillment. When you live authentically, you experience a deeper sense of peace, satisfaction, and purpose because your actions align with your inner truth.

However, living authentically can also be challenging. It often requires making difficult decisions, setting boundaries, and resisting the urge to seek external approval. We'll explore practical strategies for remaining true to yourself, even in the face of societal pressures or resistance from others.

2. The Practice of Self-Reflection

Regular self-reflection is one of the most important tools for staying aligned with your true self. There are methods for reflecting on your life, goals, and choices to ensure that they are still in alignment with your core values and vision.

Whether it's through journaling, meditation, or simply taking quiet moments to check in with yourself, self-reflection helps you stay grounded and aware of whether you're on the right track. Start to incorporate self-reflection into your daily or weekly routine and learn how to use it to course-correct when needed.

3. Trusting Your Intuition

Intuition is the inner compass that guides you toward what feels right, even when logic or external advice may tell you otherwise. Many people struggle with trusting their intuition because they've been conditioned to rely on external sources for validation. Now is the time to trust your intuition when making decisions.

Explore how intuition works, how to recognize the signals your body and mind give you when you're in alignment, and how to distinguish between intuitive insights and fear-based thinking. By learning to trust your inner guidance, you'll find it easier to stay on the path that's right for you.

4. The Power of Saying "No"

One of the most critical skills for staying aligned with your true self is the ability to say "no" to opportunities, commitments, and people that don't align with your values or goals. Discover the importance of setting boundaries and the freedom that comes from saying "no" to things that pull you off course.

Saying "no" can be difficult, especially when you fear disappointing others or missing out on potential opportunities. Learn how to confidently say "no" in a way that honors your boundaries while still maintaining respectful and positive relationships with others. Remember, every "no" creates space for a more meaningful "yes."

5. Embracing Impermanence and Change

While alignment with your true self is the key to staying on the right track, it's also important to acknowledge that you are constantly evolving. Your interests, goals, and even your values may shift over time, and that's not only okay—it's natural. Explore the importance of embracing impermanence and being open to change.

Learn how to navigate transitions with grace and flexibility and how to stay true to yourself even as your circumstances change. Remember to regularly reassess your goals and vision to ensure they still reflect who you are and what you want. This mindset of adaptability allows you to stay on the right track, even when the path forward looks different from what you initially imagined.

6. Finding Joy in the Present Moment

Staying aligned with your true self isn't just about working toward future goals—it's about finding joy, meaning, and fulfillment in the present moment. Emphasize the value of gratitude and mindfulness and how they can help you enjoy life.

Learn techniques for cultivating presence and appreciating the small moments, even as you work toward larger aspirations. By grounding yourself in the present, you can reduce anxiety about the future and experience more joy and satisfaction in your everyday life.

7. The Continuous Journey of Self-Discovery

As we close this book, it's important to recognize that staying on the right track is not a one-time achievement—it's an ongoing journey of self-discovery and self-alignment. Your journey of self-discovery and self-alignment will persist as you grow, evolve, and confront new challenges. However, by maintaining a connection to your true self, you can navigate these unforeseen turns with confidence and clarity.

Always maintain a mindset of curiosity and openness as you continue to discover more about yourself and what brings you fulfillment. Learn how to embrace the process of becoming, rather than focusing solely on reaching specific destinations.

8. Creating a Personal Manifesto

To conclude this chapter—and the book—I invite you to create your personal manifesto. This is a declaration of your values, vision, and guiding principles that will help you stay aligned with your true self as you continue on your journey. Your manifesto will serve as a compass, reminding you of what matters most and helping you make decisions that reflect your authentic self.

Begin to write your manifesto, outlining the core beliefs and values that guide you, the goals that inspire you, and the mindset you want to carry forward. This manifesto is a living document that you can revisit and revise as you grow, but it will always serve as a reminder of the path you've chosen and the person you want to be.

The journey to staying on the right track is not about reaching a final destination—it's about continuously staying aligned with your true self as you navigate life's many twists and turns. As you've learned throughout this book, the right track is a path of authenticity, reflection, growth, and resilience. It's about embracing change, trusting yourself, and cultivating relationships and environments that support your unique journey.

By staying true to your values, trusting your intuition, and remaining open to the evolving nature of life, you can create a life that is fulfilling, meaningful, and aligned with your deepest desires. As you continue forward, remember that you are the author of your own journey. Stay curious, stay courageous, and most importantly, stay true to yourself.

The right track isn't a fixed path—it's the one that allows you to be fully and authentically you.

CONCLUSION

Finding the right track in life is a journey that requires self-reflection, self-awareness, and perseverance. It's not always easy, and there will be obstacles and setbacks along the way. However, by taking the steps outlined in this book, you can gain clarity on your values and strengths, create a vision for your future, set achievable goals, and overcome obstacles to stay on track towards a fulfilling life.

Keep in mind that determining the correct path is a unique experience, and there is no universal solution. What works for one person may not work for another. It's important to stay true to yourself, listen to your intuition, and be open to adjusting your course as needed.

Throughout this journey, it's also essential to seek support from others. Seek help when needed and surround yourself with supportive people. Whether it's a mentor, a friend, or a coach, having someone to guide you and hold you accountable can make all the difference.

Finally, remember that the journey towards finding the right track is ongoing. As you grow and change, your values, strengths, and goals may shift. That's okay. The key is to stay committed to your vision and remain open to adjusting your course along the way.

By following the steps outlined in this book and staying committed to your path, you can find the right track and live a fulfilling life that aligns with your values and purpose.

Final Thoughts

As you close this book and take the next steps on your journey, remember that being on the "right track" is not about perfection or following a rigid blueprint. It's about the ongoing pursuit of living in alignment with your true self, your values, and your passions. Life is dynamic, full of change, surprises, and challenges—but with the right mindset, these moments of uncertainty can be opportunities for growth, discovery, and reinvention.

There will be times when you feel off-course or unsure, and that's okay. This is part of the human experience. What matters most is how you respond—whether you choose to pause, reflect, and realign with your deeper purpose or push forward on a path that no longer feels right for you. Always remember that it's never too late to adjust your course and rediscover what truly fulfills you.

This book has provided you with tools and insights for finding and staying on your path, but ultimately, the journey is yours. You hold the power to define what success means to you, what brings you joy, and what values guide your life. Trust in that power. Trust in your ability to navigate the twists and turns with grace, wisdom, and courage.

As you continue onward, embrace the process of self-discovery. Celebrate your small victories. Surround yourself with people who uplift and inspire you. Be kind to yourself during difficult moments and never lose sight of the fact that the journey itself is where the richness of life unfolds. There will be milestones, but the real magic lies in how you grow and evolve along the way.

Above all, remember that you are not bound by anyone else's definition of success or happiness. The track you're on is yours, and as long as it brings you closer to a life that feels authentic, meaningful, and aligned with your deepest values, you are on the right track.

Trust yourself. Stay curious. Keep moving forward, even when the path is uncertain. And always, always remain true to who you are.

About the Author

Benjamin M. Noynay is a passionate and dedicated Music Teacher and a Business Coach based in Melbourne, Australia. As a Music Teacher, Ben incorporates the principles of empowerment into his lessons, which leads to an effective collaboration with his student in a way that opens the doors of ownership, responsibility, and accountability for both of them. Once officially enrolled, you will begin a challenging yet enjoyable journey of learning music with a focused objective of achieving excellence by developing and maximizing your God-given gifts and talents and eventually converting them into skillful performances that you can share with the world.

As a Business Coach, Ben focuses on teaching and guiding his clients on how to grow their business by using the tools and resources of RIGHT Coaching Systems. He helps his clients achieve both their business and personal goals, enabling them to enjoy an abundant, well-balanced, and fulfilling lifestyle. As the founder of RIGHT Coaching Systems, Ben sets high standards for how he conducts his business based on respect, integrity, gratitude, honesty, and Trust. He believes that you can be a successful business owner and a good person at the same time. Once your coaching relationship with Ben starts, he will be there with you every step of the way until you achieve your goals.

www.ingramcontent.com/pod-product-compliance
Lightning Source LLC
Chambersburg PA
CBHW071250070526
44583CB00017B/2407